ANDREW BOVELL

Andrew Bovell's stage plays include *Speaking in Tongues*, *An Ocean Out of My Window*, *Ship of Fools*, *After Dinner*, *The Ballad of Lois Ryan* and *Holy Day*. He has collaborated on several projects including *Scenes from a Separation* (with Hannie Rayson), *Who's Afraid of the Working Class?* (with Christos Tsiolkas, Melissa Reeves, Patricia Cornelius and Irene Vela), and the feature films *Strictly Ballroom* (with Baz Luhrmann and Craig Pearce) and *Head On* (with Ana Kokkinos and Mira Robertson). His screenplay *Lantana* was based on his play *Speaking in Tongues*. The film was directed by Ray Lawrence and opened to critical acclaim in 2001, winning seven AFI awards, including Best Adapted Screenplay. He was named Screenwriter of the Year in 2002 by the London Film Critics' Circle.

Andrew Bovell

WHEN THE RAIN STOPS FALLING

NICK HERN BOOKS

London

www.nickhernbooks.co.uk

A Nick Hern Book

When the Rain Stops Falling first published in Great Britain as a paperback original in 2009 by Nick Hern Books Limited, 14 Larden Road, London W3 7ST, by arrangement with Currency Press Pty Ltd, PO Box 2287, Strawberry Hills, NSW 2012, Australia, www.currency.com.au

Reprinted 2009

When the Rain Stops Falling copyright © 2009 Andrew Bovell

Andrew Bovell has asserted his right to be identified as the author of this work

Cover image: Graham Peers (based on *Another Place* by Anthony Gormley; this is not a true representation of the work as the photograph has been altered)

Cover design: Ned Hoste, 2H

Typeset by Nick Hern Books, London

Printed and bound in Great Britain by CPI Antony Rowe, Chippenham, Wiltshire

A CIP catalogue record for this book is available from the British Library

ISBN   978 1 84842 034 2

FSC
Mixed Sources
Product group from well-managed forests and other controlled sources

Cert no. SGS-COC-2953
www.fsc.org
© 1996 Forest Stewardship Council

When the Rain Stops Falling was commissioned and first produced by Brink Productions in Australia, developed in collaboration with Hossein Valamanesh. It premiered at the Scott Theatre, University of Adelaide, on 28 February 2008, co-presented by Brink Productions, the State Theatre Company of South Australia and the 2008 Adelaide Bank Festival of Arts. The cast for this production, in order of appearance, was:

GABRIEL YORK	Neil Pigot
ELIZABETH LAW (OLDER)	Carmel Johnson
GABRIELLE YORK (YOUNGER)	Anna Lise Phillips
JOE RYAN	Paul Blackwell
GABRIELLE YORK (OLDER)	Kris McQuade
ELIZABETH LAW (YOUNGER)	Michaela Cantwell
GABRIEL LAW	Yalin Ozucelik
HENRY LAW	Neil Pigot
ANDREW PRICE	Yalin Ozucelik
MUSICIAN	Quentin Grant

Director/Dramaturg   Chris Drummond
Designer   Hossein Valamanesh
Composer   Quentin Grant
Lighting Designer   Niklas Pajanti
Video Designer   TheimaGen
Producer   Kay Jamieson

When the Rain Stops Falling received its European premiere at the Almeida Theatre, London, on 15 May 2009, with the following cast, in order of appearance:

GABRIEL YORK	Richard Hope
ELIZABETH LAW (OLDER)	Phoebe Nicholls
GABRIELLE YORK (YOUNGER)	Naomi Bentley
JOE RYAN	Simon Burke
GABRIELLE YORK (OLDER)	Leah Purcell
ELIZABETH LAW (YOUNGER)	Lisa Dillon
GABRIEL LAW	Tom Mison
HENRY LAW	Jonathan Cullen
ANDREW PRICE	Sargon Yelda

Director   Michael Attenborough
Designer   Miriam Buether
Lighting Designer   Colin Grenfell
Video Designer   Lorna Heavey
Composer   Stephen Warbeck
Sound Designer   Paul Arditti
Movement   Imogen Knight

A Family Tree

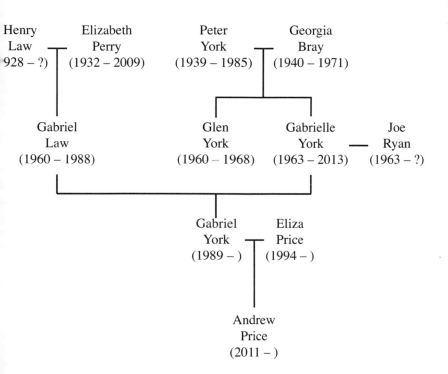

Characters and Settings

The play takes place between 1959 and 2039

1960s
A small flat in London
HENRY LAW, *40s*
ELIZABETH LAW, *30s*

1988
The same flat in London
ELIZABETH LAW, *56*
GABRIEL LAW, *28, her son*

1988
The Coorong on the southern coast of Australia, and Uluru
GABRIELLE YORK, *24*
GABRIEL LAW, *28*

2013
A small flat in Adelaide and a nearby park
GABRIELLE YORK, *50*
JOE RYAN, *50*

2039
A small flat in Alice Springs
GABRIEL YORK, *50, the son of Gabriel Law and Gabrielle York*
ANDREW PRICE, *28, the son of Gabriel York*

*The original Brink production in Adelaide used seven actors.
The roles of Henry Law and Gabriel York were played by the
same actor, as were the roles of Gabriel Law and Andrew Price.
As a result, Gabriel Law did not appear as one of the ancestors
in the final scene of the play. The Almeida production in London
used nine actors, allowing the character of Gabriel Law to
appear in the final scene.*

Let us begin with

A Steady Fall of Rain

GABRIEL YORK *wears a raincoat and stands beneath a black umbrella.*

People pass him by. Back and forth. Back and forth. Like GABRIEL, *they carry umbrellas and wear raincoats. Their heads are bent against the relentless weather and against their relentless lives. Back and forth. Back and forth. Until in unison they stop.*

And GABRIEL *opens his mouth and screams.*

And a woman falls to her knees in the street.

And a fish falls from the sky and lands at GABRIEL's *feet.*

Black.

Gabriel York's Room

Alice Springs 2039

GABRIEL YORK *stands holding the fish.*

GABRIEL. I do not believe in God. I do not believe in miracles. I cannot explain this.

It began with a phone call. It was Friday evening. About 10 p.m. Which was unusual. The phone rarely rings and never at that hour. I was reading. As I do before bed. A history. *The Decline and Fall of the American Empire 1975–2015.* I am fascinated by the past. Which may, at least in part, explain the fish.

I have not seen a fish like this for many years. Not since I was a boy. I mean, I have seen pictures of them but not one in the flesh. They are, after all, or at least they are meant to be, extinct.

Though I have heard rumours that they are still occasionally caught and served, secretly, in the most exclusive of restaurants, but only for the select few and only for those who can pay. If I was to purchase such a fish, if purchasing such a fish as this was still possible for the man in the street, it would cost me a year's wages. I could never dream of affording such a delicacy. If such a delicacy still existed.

He looks at the fish.

Which strangely, it seems to do.

He lays the fish on the table.

I hesitated before answering the phone. Wrong number, I thought. Surely. Who would call me? Me? At this hour?

It was my son. Andrew.

The name was his mother's choice. I had wanted to call him Joe. After a man I once knew. Joe was a good man. He told me he only swore once in his life and that was the day he met my mother. And he was always losing his hat. He liked to walk and one day he went for a walk and never came back so it was probably better that it was Andrew and not Joe.

I haven't seen Andrew for many years. I left when he was a boy. It was cowardly of me, I know. But I was not the fathering type and to be perfectly honest I thought the boy had a better chance without me. I sent money, of course. When I could. And a card. Now and then. For the first few years. I'm not proud of it.

Anyway there he was... this Andrew, this son of mine, on the phone at 10 p.m. on a Friday night. 'Hello? Is this Gabriel York? It's Andrew here. Your son. I hope you don't mind me calling you like this. I hope you don't mind. It's just that I'm in Alice. And I was wondering if I could see

you. Dad?' Only it went more like. 'Hello?... Is this...
Gabriel York?... It's Andrew here... Your son... I hope you
don't mind me calling you like this... I hope you don't
mind... It's just that... I'm in Alice... And ... I was
wondering if I could see you?... Dad?'

And my mind was racing, trying to stay calm, trying to take
each piece of information in and just as I came to terms with
one extraordinary fact, such as 'It's Andrew', he would say
something else, like 'Your son', until I felt unable to reply
and the longer I said nothing, the harder it became to say
anything at all and so I hung up. And returned to my book.
The Decline and Fall of the American Empire... 1975–2015.

I can't imagine what he thought of me.

I tried to concentrate on the page I was reading but found
myself rereading the same line over and over again, its
meaning escaping me, when I tasted something salty in the
corner of my mouth and realised that I was crying. The tears
were falling from my eyes, rolling across my cheeks and
gathering in the corners of my mouth. And of course I knew
I was crying because of him, hearing his voice, the voice of
an adult now when I could only remember the child but it
also felt like I was crying for so much more.

So I lifted the receiver and recalled the last number.
'Andrew?... I'm sorry. That was unforgivable of me.' And
he didn't say anything and I realised that he was crying too
and I wondered whether his tears tasted as bitter as mine. I
hoped not... 'I'm so sorry,' I said... 'I'd like to see you very
much. Why don't you come for lunch tomorrow?'

And as soon as I had given him my address and hung up I
knew that it was a mistake. Lunch? What was I thinking?
What would I give him? I can hardly feed myself, let alone a
son I haven't seen for what... twenty years? What do you
serve for lunch in circumstances like that? I mean, lunch
hardly seems the point.

And besides, what will he think of me? Me? I mean, what
will he think of the clothes I wear? My suit? Which looks

alright from a distance but up close is quite shabby and old-fashioned. Second-hand. Or third perhaps. But certainly not purchased new. And my shoes, worn at the toes and down at the heel. And will he notice that I don't wear socks? Not if I don't sit down or cross my legs. If I remain standing my son won't know that I don't wear socks.

And what will he think of my room? It isn't much. It isn't anything at all. A one-room bedsit on the twelfth floor. Not the kind of place a father should live. Surely. And it needs a paint and the carpets are worn. And it's dirty. To be perfectly honest, it's filthy. In the corners and on the window sills and the ceilings. Layers of dust and dirt and grime and dead insects. Years of neglect. And will he notice the smell? Of a man who lives alone. I mean, I wash. Of course I wash. But not often. There hasn't been the need. Until now.

And so I began to clean it. The room. That night. A bucket of hot water and soap suds. I washed the walls, the ceilings, even the light fittings were scrubbed. I washed the door handles and the light switches and the dark corners behind the furniture. I scrubbed the table and the floor and polished the windows. I dusted the books and the lampshade and even took to the grouting between the tiles with a toothbrush. And by morning, when I had finally finished I looked around and it looked exactly the same. So I found an old tin of leftover paint in the cupboard. White. Or off-white. Pure white being too stark. Like a hospital. And I pulled the furniture to the centre of the room and covered it with sheets. I took the pictures off the walls. I took the books from the bookcases. And I painted. And I painted. And I painted. And when I finished I looked around and it still looked exactly the same. Only whiter.

And I began to feel angry. Why did he call? Why is he doing this? What does he want from me? Money? Is that it? Does he think I'm worth something? Does he think I owe him something? And as I'm thinking these thoughts I'm also thinking how terrible, how irrational, how baseless, how shameful it was to have these thoughts. How shameful I am. How appalling I am.

What kind of man am I?

And then I realised that it was Saturday. He would be here in an hour and there was nothing to eat. I wanted it to be special. I wanted to feed my son something substantial. Something nourishing. Something to make up for all those meals I failed to provide. And there was nothing in the cupboard. So I went out. And it was raining. Pouring. It has been for days. Still is. The river is swollen and threatening to break its banks. Two of the bridges have already been closed. And I didn't know whether I would make the shops or even what I would buy if I got there. And it was too much. I just couldn't manage it. I couldn't look after him then. And I still can't. I just can't. And I screamed. I just screamed. I opened my mouth and screamed and a fish fell out of the sky and landed at my feet.

And it still smelt of the sea.

I don't believe in God. I don't believe in miracles. I cannot begin to explain how a fish can fall from the sky in a town surrounded by desert. I cannot begin to explain this. But it is truly the most wonderful thing that has ever happened to me... And now all that is left for me to do is to put the fish in the oven and wait for the knock on the door.

I know why he is coming. My son. I know what he wants. He wants what all young men want from their fathers. He wants to know who he is. Where he comes from. Where he belongs. And for the life of me I don't know what I will tell him. For whilst I know a great deal about the decline and fall of the American Empire, my own past escapes me. All I have are a few fragments, a few bits and pieces I found in an old suitcase after my mother's death. I don't know what they mean. I don't know how to make sense of them. I stopped trying to years ago.

The past is a mystery.

GABRIEL *looks at the fish*.

And yet, perhaps it will be easier to explain than the fish.

Rooms

ELIZABETH LAW, *56, enters and shakes the water from her black umbrella. She is the woman who fell in the street. She closes her umbrella and hangs it on a hook. She removes her raincoat and hangs it beside the umbrella. She crosses to the window and stares down into the street as*

GABRIELLE YORK, *24, enters and shakes the water from her black umbrella. She closes it and hangs it on a hook. She removes her raincoat and hangs it beside the umbrella. She crosses to the window and stares down into the street as* ELIZABETH *moves from the window into an adjacent bathroom. We can hear her urinating as*

JOE RYAN, *50, enters and shakes the water from his black umbrella. He closes it and hangs it on a hook. He removes his raincoat and hangs it beside the umbrella. He crosses to the window and stares down into the street as* GABRIELLE *moves from the window into an adjacent bathroom as* ELIZABETH *enters from the bathroom and stops, lost in a moment's thought. We can hear* GABRIELLE *urinating as*

GABRIELLE YORK, *50, enters and shakes the water from her black umbrella. She closes it and hangs it on a hook. She removes her raincoat and hangs it beside the umbrella. She crosses to the window and stares down into the street as* JOE *moves from the window and enters the adjacent bathroom as the* YOUNGER GABRIELLE *enters from the bathroom and stops, lost in a moment's thought as* ELIZABETH *takes a bowl and a spoon and fills her bowl with soup from a large pot on the stove. We can hear* JOE *urinating as*

ELIZABETH LAW, *30s, enters and shakes the water from her black umbrella. She closes it and hangs it on a hook. She removes her raincoat and hangs it beside the umbrella. She crosses to the window and stares down into the street as the* OLDER GABRIELLE *moves from the window into the adjacent bathroom as* JOE *enters from the bathroom and stops, lost in a moment's thought and then he touches his head as if he has lost his hat as the* YOUNGER GABRIELLE *takes a bowl and spoon and fills her bowl with soup as the* OLDER ELIZABETH *takes a place at the table and proceeds to eat her soup alone. We can hear the* OLDER GABRIELLE *urinating as*

GABRIEL LAW, *28, enters and shakes the water from his black umbrella. He closes it and hangs it on a hook. He removes his raincoat and hangs it beside the umbrella. He crosses to the window and stares down into the street as the* YOUNGER ELIZABETH *moves from the window and enters the adjacent bathroom as the* OLDER GABRIELLE *enters from the bathroom and stops, lost in a moment's thought as* JOE *takes a bowl and spoon and fills his bowl with soup as the* YOUNGER GABRIELLE *takes a place at the table and proceeds to eat her soup alone as does the* OLDER ELIZABETH. *We can hear the* YOUNGER ELIZABETH *urinating as*

HENRY LAW, *40s, enters and shakes the water from his black umbrella. He closes it and hangs it on a hook. He removes his raincoat and hangs it beside the umbrella. Then he removes his hat and hangs it over the raincoat. He crosses to the window and stares down into the street as* GABRIEL *moves from the window and enters the adjacent bathroom as the* YOUNGER ELIZABETH *enters from the bathroom and stops, lost in a moment's thought. She places her hand on her belly as the* OLDER GABRIELLE *takes a bowl and spoon and fills her bowl with soup as* JOE *takes his place at the table and eats his soup alone as do the* YOUNGER GABRIELLE *and the* OLDER ELIZABETH. *We can hear* GABRIEL *urinating.*

HENRY *moves from the window and enters the adjacent bathroom as* GABRIEL *enters from the bathroom and stops, lost in a moment's thought as the* YOUNGER ELIZABETH *takes a bowl and spoon and fills her bowl with soup as the* OLDER GABRIELLE *takes her place at the table and proceeds to eat her soup alone as do* JOE, *the* YOUNGER GABRIELLE *and the* OLDER ELIZABETH. *We can hear* HENRY *urinating.*

Then HENRY *enters from the bathroom and stops, lost in a moment's thought as* GABRIEL *takes a spoon and bowl and fills his bowl with soup as the* YOUNGER ELIZABETH *takes her place at the table and proceeds to eat her soup alone as do the* OLDER GABRIELLE, JOE, *the* YOUNGER GABRIELLE *and the* OLDER ELIZABETH.

Then HENRY *takes a bowl and spoon and fills his bowl with soup as* GABRIEL *takes his place at the table and proceeds to eat his soup alone as do the* YOUNGER ELIZABETH, *the* OLDER GABRIELLE, JOE, *the* YOUNGER GABRIELLE *and the* OLDER ELIZABETH.

Then HENRY *takes his place at the table and proceeds to eat his soup, alone.*

And now all seven are at the table, alone and eating their soup in silence. And the movement of their spoons to their mouths slowly falls into a shared rhythm until the OLDER ELIZABETH *looks up from her bowl.*

ELIZABETH. How's the soup?

And then they all rise and exit except for the OLDER ELIZABETH *and* GABRIEL LAW.

And we are in

Elizabeth Law's Room

London 1988

GABRIEL. Fine.

ELIZABETH. I wasn't sure what to give you.

GABRIEL. No.

ELIZABETH. It's just that when you called you said you'd be here for lunch.

GABRIEL. Actually, I said I'd be here about twelve and you said why not come for lunch.

ELIZABETH. And you said fine.

GABRIEL. But I said don't go to any trouble.

ELIZABETH. Nevertheless. (*Beat.*) Did you get very wet?

GABRIEL. I had my umbrella.

ELIZABETH. Well yes, it's the day for it. Still, there are people drowning in Bangladesh so we shouldn't complain.

GABRIEL. It wasn't a complaint. (*Beat.*) Have you done something?

ELIZABETH. What?

GABRIEL. Changed something.

ELIZABETH. I've painted.

GABRIEL. By yourself?

ELIZABETH. No. I had a man in.

GABRIEL. Could you afford that?

ELIZABETH. I had some paint left over.

GABRIEL. But the labour?

ELIZABETH. I had a little put away.

GABRIEL. I could have helped you.

ELIZABETH. What? With the money.

GABRIEL. Well yes, if you needed it.

ELIZABETH. But I had a little put away.

GABRIEL. I could have done the painting then.

ELIZABETH. Well… yes.

GABRIEL. You should have asked.

ELIZABETH. I didn't think of it.

GABRIEL. Well, next time.

ELIZABETH. Next time?

GABRIEL. Next time you paint.

ELIZABETH. Well, that won't be for a while.

GABRIEL. I know but... Well.

The YOUNGER ELIZABETH *enters. She shakes the water from her black umbrella. She closes it and hangs it on a hook. She removes her raincoat and hangs it beside the umbrella. She crosses to the window and looks down into the street.*

ELIZABETH (OLDER). There's a new fishmonger in the high street and after your call I thought, well, what will I give him? He's such a fussy eater. Always has been. Do you remember? What a fussy eater you were?

GABRIEL. No.

ELIZABETH. You ate like a bird. You picked at your food. You didn't eat. You picked. I'm surprised you didn't starve to death. And I mean, I don't know what you like or don't like, your tastes are a mystery to me, so I walked down the street thinking I might be inspired, in this weather, would you believe?

GABRIEL. But I said don't go to any trouble.

ELIZABETH. But you had to eat.

The YOUNGER ELIZABETH *turns from the window and then stops, lost in a moment's thought.*

Anyway, I was on the high street and I saw the new shop. It had only just opened and it had a display in the window of this most beautiful fish. I mean, I don't know what it was. It was certainly not a cod or a haddock. God knows where it came from and I thought, well, what about fish? Well, not fish. But fish soup. Something light. He won't want something heavy. Not at lunchtime. Not with his appetite.

The YOUNGER ELIZABETH *proceeds to take a bowl and a spoon and fill her bowl with soup from a large pot on the stove.*

You do eat fish?

GABRIEL. Not often.

ELIZABETH. They say it's good for you. And it's simple. Easy to prepare. Especially for one.

GABRIEL. Anyway… how are you, Mum?

The YOUNGER ELIZABETH *takes a place at the table and proceeds to eat her soup.*

ELIZABETH. Oh well, you know.

GABRIEL. What does that mean?

ELIZABETH. I never know how to answer that, Gabriel. I'm never sure whether people, when they ask it, want me to tell them the truth or whether they just want me to go through the motions. If it's the latter you want then I'm very well, thank you. I've been a little tired and I'm fighting off a cold but no, on the whole I'm fine.

GABRIEL. Actually I'd prefer the truth.

The YOUNGER ELIZABETH *stops eating.*

ELIZABETH (OLDER). I had a fall, Gabriel.

Beat. HENRY *enters.*

ELIZABETH (YOUNGER). There you are.

GABRIEL *and the* OLDER ELIZABETH *exit.*

And we are in

The Same Room

London 1959

As they speak, HENRY *shakes the water from his umbrella and hangs it on a hook, removes his raincoat and hangs it beside the umbrella and then removes a hat and hangs it over the raincoat.*

HENRY. What unbelievable weather.

ELIZABETH. Torrential.

HENRY. In London!

ELIZABETH. Are you very wet?

HENRY. Drenched. Still, there are people drowning in East Pakistan so we shouldn't complain.

ELIZABETH. There's soup in the pot.

HENRY (*crossing to the window*). Wonderful.

ELIZABETH. It's fish, I'm afraid.

HENRY *looks down into the street below.*

There's a new fishmonger in the high street. Lovely man. Greek. Do anything for you.

HENRY *moves from the window and enters the adjacent bathroom.*

I was walking past thinking what would we eat when I saw this huge fish in the window, God knows where it came from, and I thought, well, what about fish? Well, not fish but fish soup. I only had to boil some heads and add some herbs and vegetables, neither of which I had, so it's just the heads I'm afraid, but there you are. Actually, there's something I should tell you.

HENRY (*entering*). I was reading this piece on the way home. (*He proceeds to the stove and fills his bowl with soup.*) 'The

Year Without a Summer.' 1816. Heavy frosts and snowstorms sweep across North America and Europe in the middle of June.

ELIZABETH. Heavens!

HENRY (*taking his place at the table*). Followed by weeks of unseasonable rain. Crops fail. Prices soar. Famine in China due to the failure of the rice crop. Food riots in England and France. Absolute disaster.

He tastes the soup.

ELIZABETH. It might need something.

HENRY. Salt perhaps?

ELIZABETH. Food bores me, Henry. If it wasn't necessary I wouldn't eat.

HENRY (*pushing his bowl aside*). But the greatest acts of civil disobedience occur in Switzerland.

ELIZABETH. Switzerland?

HENRY. Well, exactly. The whole thing was caused by the eruption of Mount Tambora in Indonesia the year before. In Italy there were reports of red snow. People ran through the streets screaming, 'The heavens are bleeding.' They thought it was the end of the world.

ELIZABETH. Well, I imagine it was for some.

HENRY. Two hundred thousand dead in Europe alone. Uncounted more in Asia and Russia. And in America hundreds of thousands flee west trying to escape the weather. It shifted whole populations, Beth. It changed the course of history. The weather! And it made me think just how helpless we are when the weather turns against us. All our science. All our knowledge. All our magnificent endeavour amounts to very little in the face of bad weather.

ELIZABETH. Do you think so? I mean, the fact that 1817 followed 1816 suggests a degree of resilience worth considering, Henry. We survived. Or most of us did. And anyway Mary Shelley wrote *Frankenstein* in Switzerland in 1816. So there you are. It will take more than a spot of bad weather to silence the human mind. Actually, I know why the greatest acts of civil disobedience occurred in Switzerland.

HENRY. Why?

ELIZABETH. Because the more ordered a society, the less able it is to cope with chaos. Whilst a naturally chaotic one such as Italy can face a fair degree of disaster before the people actually start to panic.

HENRY. Your mind, Beth.

ELIZABETH. It makes sense, Henry.

HENRY. I fell in love with you because of your mind.

ELIZABETH. What were you looking at… before… at the window when you came in?

HENRY. A woman.

ELIZABETH. Red umbrella. Herringbone jacket.

HENRY. How did you know?

ELIZABETH. I saw her from the window.

HENRY. What was she doing?

ELIZABETH. Talking to you.

HENRY. Well yes, she followed me all the way from the station.

ELIZABETH. What did she want?

HENRY. She said she had my hat.

ELIZABETH. Do you have a hat?

HENRY. Well, exactly! She said she saw me leave it on the seat on the train. And as she was getting off anyway, she thought that she would take the hat and return it to me. But I walk fast. You know how fast I walk, and she couldn't keep up.

ELIZABETH. The heels wouldn't have helped.

HENRY. And she said that she was calling… 'Excuse me…
  your hat.'

ELIZABETH. Well, didn't you hear her?

HENRY. Well yes, I heard her but I didn't pay it any attention.

ELIZABETH. Why not?

HENRY. Because I didn't know she was talking to me. I mean,
  I just thought she was some woman chasing a man who had
  lost his hat.

ELIZABETH. Well, that's exactly what she was, Henry.

HENRY. But I don't wear a hat.

ELIZABETH. No, you don't. Normally.

  JOE *enters. He shakes the water from his umbrella and
  hangs it on a hook. He removes his raincoat and hangs it on
  a hook beside the umbrella.*

HENRY. So eventually she catches up with me and she was
  breathless, the poor thing, and I'm thinking, quite wrongly as
  it turns out, why do they always choose me?

  JOE *moves to the window and looks down to the street below.*

  And she's saying, 'I have your hat. You left your hat on the
  train.' And she's thrusting it into my hands and I find myself
  saying, I mean, the words just fall out of my mouth, I say,
  'Thank you.'

  Then JOE *moves into the adjacent bathroom.*

ELIZABETH. But it wasn't your hat.

HENRY. I know.

ELIZABETH. Why didn't you tell her?

HENRY. Because she had gone to so much trouble and seemed
  so pleased with herself for returning the hat. I mean, she'd
  run nearly a mile to give it to me and probably ruined her
  heels in the process. I just didn't want to disappoint her.

ELIZABETH. So what happened to the hat?

HENRY (*crossing to the hook and retrieving the hat*). It's here. Hanging on the hook. (*He takes the hat and puts it on.*) Like it was mine.

ELIZABETH. But it's not yours.

JOE *comes out of the bathroom and stops, remembering his hat.*

HENRY. No.

ELIZABETH. Then whose hat is it?

JOE *touches his head and realises that his hat's not there.*

HENRY. I have no idea.

ELIZABETH. Well.

HENRY. Exactly.

ELIZABETH. There's something I should tell you, Henry.

HENRY. What?

ELIZABETH. I'm pregnant.

Beat.

HENRY. Right.

ELIZABETH. I know.

HENRY. Well.

ELIZABETH. Unexpected.

HENRY. A little.

ELIZABETH. Will we manage, because I can –

HENRY. No.

ELIZABETH. Because I don't mind –

HENRY. We'll manage.

ELIZABETH. It's just that –

HENRY. Of course we'll manage.

ELIZABETH. It's just that –

HENRY. We'll manage, Beth.

ELIZABETH. Yes but it wasn't meant to happen, was it?
Perhaps ten years ago. When I was ready. But not now,
Henry. Because I've got on. I've made a life without it and,
to be frank, to be perfectly honest, I'm just not sure I want it.

The OLDER GABRIELLE *enters and shakes the water from
her umbrella.*

JOE. There you are.

HENRY *and* ELIZABETH *exit.*

And we are in

Joe Ryan and Gabrielle York's Room

Adelaide 2013

GABRIELLE. Where?

She closes the umbrella and hangs it on the hook.

JOE. By the door. Hanging up your umbrella.

GABRIELLE. Am I? I thought I was by the window scratching
my bum.

*She removes her raincoat and hangs it on a hook beside the
umbrella.*

JOE. I've lost my hat.

GABRIELLE. Terrible weather.

JOE. Did you get wet?

GABRIELLE. I had my umbrella.

JOE. You've been out.

GABRIELLE. I went for a walk.

JOE. Where to?

GABRIELLE. Still there are people drowning…

She trails away.

JOE. What?

GABRIELLE. In Bangladesh. There are people drowning in Bangladesh.

JOE. Are there?

GABRIELLE. It's just what people say, Joe. A figure of speech.

JOE. I've never heard it.

GABRIELLE. Was that lightning? Did you see it?

JOE. No.

GABRIELLE. Listen.

Sure enough, a rumble of thunder. She moves to the window.

I hate nights like this. When I was a kid they would frighten me. Still do… On nights like this, ships are lost at sea.

JOE. There's soup in the pot. (*He takes a bowl and a spoon and fills the bowl with soup from a large pot on the stove.*) It's fish… They say it's good for you. Good for the brain. Not sure what it does exactly but they say we should have it three times a week at least. Not sure I could eat it that often but I thought it was worth a try.

JOE places the bowl of soup on the table.

GABRIELLE. Did Gabriel call?

JOE. No, love.

GABRIELLE. Are you sure? He might have left a message.

JOE. I've checked… there's no message. (*Beat.*) Come and have some soup.

GABRIELLE. What kind of soup?

JOE. Fish.

She moves to the table, takes a place and proceeds to eat her soup.

GABRIELLE. Somebody said it's very good for you. Good for the brain. You should have it three times a week or something.

JOE. That's right.

GABRIELLE. It tastes like the sea.

The YOUNGER GABRIELLE *enters and shakes the water from her umbrella. She hangs it on a hook and removes her raincoat and hangs it on the hook beside it. She moves to the window and looks out.*

What's happening to me, Joe?

JOE. Nothing, love. You're wandering a bit, that's all. You're not sure if it's today or tomorrow or yesterday. And who can blame you for that. They're all much the same.

GABRIELLE. Hold my hand.

JOE takes her hand.

I won't have it… You're not to hold on for ever.

JOE. I have to go out for a bit. See if I can find that hat.

GABRIELLE. What hat?

JOE. I lost my hat.

GABRIELLE. Terrible weather.

JOE. Did you get wet?

GABRIELLE. I had my umbrella.

JOE. You've been out.

GABRIELLE. I went for a walk.

JOE. Where to?

GABRIELLE. The shops.

JOE. What for?

GABRIELLE. Cigarettes.

JOE. You don't smoke.

GABRIELLE. I do.

JOE. You do not.

GABRIELLE. I bloody do.

JOE. Well, I didn't know.

GABRIELLE. Well, there are a lot of things you don't know. A lot of things about me. Parts of me that you don't know.

JOE. I should find that hat. (*He takes his raincoat and umbrella.*) I won't be long.

He exits.

GABRIELLE (OLDER). There are parts of me you've never touched.

GABRIEL LAW *enters and the* OLDER GABRIELLE *exits.*

And we are in

A Roadhouse

On the Coorong 1988

GABRIEL *sees the* YOUNGER GABRIELLE *at the window.*

GABRIEL. Hello.

GABRIELLE. Shit… You frightened me.

GABRIEL. I'm sorry.

GABRIELLE. Where did you come from?

GABRIEL. I just pulled up… I'm driving through the Coorong.

GABRIELLE. What for?

GABRIEL. To see it, I suppose. (*Beat.*) Terrible weather. Still, there are people drowning in Bangladesh so we shouldn't complain.

GABRIELLE. You're English.

GABRIEL. Yes… Is that alright?

GABRIELLE. A tourist?

GABRIEL. Of sorts.

GABRIELLE. Are there?

GABRIEL. Are there…?

GABRIELLE. People drowning in Bangladesh?

GABRIEL. No. It's just a figure of speech. It's something my mother says. Though they often do. Each monsoon. But they're not at the moment. At least I hope not.

GABRIELLE. Do you want something… to eat, I mean?

GABRIEL. What have you got?

GABRIELLE. Soup.

GABRIEL. What sort of soup?

GABRIELLE. Fish. (*Beat.*) You don't like fish soup?

GABRIEL. The last time I had it I threw up. I was on a bus going home after visiting my mother. It came without warning and with such force that it landed on a skinhead sitting on the seat in front of me. He had fish soup all through his mohawk so he dragged me into the aisle and beat the crap out of me. Not one person stood up to help. They all looked the other way. Even the driver. But that's London for you. I'm not sure what caused me to be so ill… the fish soup or seeing my mother.

GABRIELLE. That's not a very nice thing to say about your mother.

GABRIEL. It's a complicated relationship.

GABRIELLE. I can do you a toasted sandwich if you like.

GABRIEL. I would, thank you... Tomato and cheese.

GABRIELLE. You don't want ham?

GABRIEL. No.

GABRIELLE. You sure?

GABRIEL. I'm vegetarian. (*Beat.*) What?

GABRIELLE. I'll get your sandwich.

She goes to leave.

GABRIEL. And do you have a room?

GABRIELLE. How long are you staying?

GABRIEL. Not sure. A day or two.

GABRIELLE. I'll have to make one up. We don't get people down here this time of year.

GABRIEL. Why not?

GABRIELLE. The weather.

GABRIEL. But it's beautiful here.

GABRIELLE. Do you think?

GABRIEL. I've never seen anything like it.

GABRIELLE. I think it's the ugliest place in the world.

GABRIEL. Did you grow up here?

GABRIELLE. Yes.

GABRIEL. Then that's why. But if you look at it through the eyes of a stranger you'll see what I see.

GABRIELLE. It's still just sandhills and water and bird shit on your car.

GABRIEL. I come from London. I think that's the ugliest place in the world. Or if not the ugliest it's certainly the loneliest.

GABRIELLE. You can walk along the beach here for five days and not see anyone.

GABRIEL. I know. It's brilliant.

GABRIELLE. It's killing me.

GABRIEL. Leave.

GABRIELLE. I'm going to.

GABRIEL. As soon as you do you'll want to come back.

GABRIELLE. I want to meet people.

GABRIEL. You've met me.

GABRIELLE. What's your name?

GABRIEL. Gabriel.

GABRIELLE. It's not.

GABRIEL. It is. What's yours?

GABRIELLE. Gabrielle.

GABRIEL. What are the chances of that?

GABRIELLE. Funny name for a bloke.

GABRIEL. Do you think so?

GABRIELLE. It is down here.

GABRIEL. It means strong man of God.

GABRIELLE. I thought it was French.

GABRIEL. No, it's biblical. Gabriel was the archangel.

GABRIELLE. Are you an angel, Gabriel?

GABRIEL. No. Flesh and blood.

GABRIELLE. Were your parents religious?

GABRIEL. My mother's an atheist. A communist once, I think, judging by her library. No, she just liked the name.

GABRIELLE. So did mine. But she thought it was French. Exotic. She wanted me to be different.

GABRIEL. Are you different?

GABRIELLE. No. Not really… Maybe.

GABRIEL. How?

GABRIELLE. You'll have to find out. I'll get your sandwich.

She turns to go. He doesn't want her to leave. Ever.

GABRIEL. Are yours religious? Your parents?

GABRIELLE. They were. Catholic.

GABRIEL. Lapsed?

GABRIELLE. Dead.

GABRIEL. Oh, right.

GABRIELLE. Mum drowned herself in the ocean when I was seven and Dad put a bullet through his head three years ago. (*Beat.*) It's the place. Things like that happen here. That's why I have to get away… Take a seat. I'll get your sandwich.

GABRIELLE *exits as* GABRIEL *takes his place at the table as he was at lunch at his mother's flat as the* OLDER ELIZABETH *enters.*

GABRIEL. Where? Where did you fall?

And we are in

Elizabeth Law's Room

London 1988

ELIZABETH (OLDER). In the street. When I was out getting your fish. Silly really to have been out. In weather like this.

GABRIEL. Are you alright?

ELIZABETH. I grazed my knees, that's all. And tore my stockings. A man helped me to my feet. Lovely of him. Because they don't bother these days, do they? Most men. I blame Thatcher. Such a cruel woman.

GABRIEL. I thought you voted for her.

ELIZABETH. Thatcher? No. Why would you think that?

GABRIEL. I'm not sure. I just assumed…

ELIZABETH. Assumed what?

GABRIEL. I'm sorry you fell.

ELIZABETH. Why? You didn't push me.

GABRIEL. Then why do I feel like I did?

Beat.

ELIZABETH. It's every woman's worst fear, of course. Of a certain age. A fall.

GABRIEL. But you're not old.

ELIZABETH. No. But I am alone. And sometimes they can seem like the same thing.

GABRIEL. You don't think your drinking might have something to do with it?

ELIZABETH. Do you like the colour?

GABRIEL. Of the walls?

ELIZABETH. No, Gabriel. Of the sky. Do you like the colour of the sky? Yes, I'm talking about the walls.

GABRIEL. Well, they're white, aren't they?

ELIZABETH. Off-white. Pure white is too stark. Like a hospital.

GABRIEL. But it's the same as it's always been.

ELIZABETH. Well, I had paint left over. I thought I should use it.

GABRIEL. I was going through some old boxes recently.

ELIZABETH. Don't. Don't come into my home and judge me.

GABRIEL. I'm sorry.

ELIZABETH. This is my home.

GABRIEL. It's just that I worry about you.

ELIZABETH. Do you?

GABRIEL. Yes… I care about you, Mum.

ELIZABETH. Well, don't.

GABRIEL. Don't care about you?

ELIZABETH. Don't make a fuss, Gabriel. I'm perfectly
capable of caring for myself.

GABRIEL. I was thinking about my father recently. (*Beat.*) And
I know we've tried to have this conversation before.

ELIZABETH. Right.

GABRIEL. What?

ELIZABETH. I had hoped that you had come simply to see me.

GABRIEL. I have.

ELIZABETH. No, Gabriel. You haven't. You have come
because there is something you want.

GABRIEL. Is it such a bad thing to want?

ELIZABETH. No. But it's not something I can give you. I don't
know what happened to your father. He left. Presumably
because he was unhappy. But ultimately it was not
something I could prevent.

GABRIEL. It's curious that he never attempted to make contact.
I mean, I was his son.

ELIZABETH. The fact that you were his son was of little
consequence to him… I'm not trying to be cruel.

GABRIEL. Aren't you?

ELIZABETH. He didn't care about you, Gabriel. He didn't care about me. He cared only for himself. The man was of little consequence and he went away. What more can I possibly tell you?

GABRIEL. I was going through some old boxes recently.

ELIZABETH. Would you like more soup?

GABRIEL. I think if I ate any more I would be ill.

ELIZABETH. You didn't like it.

GABRIEL. I'm vegetarian, Mum. You know that.

ELIZABETH. But this is fish.

GABRIEL. All the same... I don't eat it.

ELIZABETH. Well, I can't be responsible for what you do and don't eat.

GABRIEL. No, you can't.

The YOUNGER ELIZABETH *enters with a pile of nappies and begins to fold them at the table.*

But I was going through some old boxes recently. Having a clean-out. Or trying to. My flat's become so cramped. I can hardly move. It's just a one-bedroom. More a bedsit really. You should visit. If you want... So I was going through all these boxes. Finding all these things. I keep everything, you see. I don't know why. All these things from the past. Things I should have thrown out years ago. Perhaps I will. Have a good throw-out. Start again. What do you think, Mum? Start again? We could... I don't know why I haven't got rid of them before, my childhood toys and football trophies and class photos and all the birthday cards I made you, I mean, I don't know why I can't part with them. It's so unlike you. You don't keep anything. Not even memories.

ELIZABETH. I keep old paint.

GABRIEL. Well yes, but apart from old paint you let it all go and I envy that.

ELIZABETH. Nostalgia bores me, Gabriel.

GABRIEL. I used to collect stamps. Do you remember?

ELIZABETH. No.

GABRIEL. I have stamps from all over the world, from countries that don't even exist any more, all neatly laid out in albums. A different album for every country and three of every stamp. One to keep, one to replace it in case it is damaged, and one to swap should the opportunity arise.

ELIZABETH. You should have it valued. It might be worth something.

GABRIEL. So I was searching through these stamp albums when I found a newspaper clipping tucked into the back of one of them. It was dated some time in 1970. So I must have been, I don't know, ten, and I had forgotten about it of course, as you do. You forget these things. But it was a report about the disappearance of a man at Ayers Rock, in Australia. Do you remember it?

She is silent.

A man was seen climbing the rock at dusk by campers. Several people passed him on the way down and warned him to turn back. It was getting dark. You're not allowed up there at night. It's dangerous. Easy to fall. But he wouldn't listen. He continued to climb… He was described as being a man of fair complexion with an English accent. Anyway, he failed to return. And despite an extensive search, no trace of him was ever found. (*Beat.*) I mean, I'm sure there's an explanation but I remember being taken by this all the same, wondering what happened to the man and whether somehow he was still up there, as though he had slipped into some kind of parallel time frame. You know how children's minds think.

ELIZABETH. No, not really.

GABRIEL. It's funny the things you remember, but I remember searching through your sewing drawer for the good scissors, which you hated me using to cut paper with. And I knew I shouldn't be doing it but children will always look where they're not meant to. And I found them. (*Beat*.) The scissors. And I cut out the article and tucked it into the back of this stamp album... And I must have forgotten about it, and there it was all these years later, and I find myself thinking about this man again, this fair-skinned Englishman, and wondering who he was... and what happened to him.

HENRY *enters*.

ELIZABETH (YOUNGER). There you are.

GABRIEL LAW *and the* OLDER ELIZABETH *exit*.

And we are in

The Same Room

London 1962

HENRY. I've lost my umbrella.

ELIZABETH. Where?

HENRY. I've left it on the train.

ELIZABETH. But didn't you notice it was raining when you got off?

HENRY. Strangely no. Not straight away. And by the time I did, the train had left the platform.

ELIZABETH. There's soup in the pot.

HENRY. Right.

ELIZABETH. It's fish, I'm afraid.

HENRY. Terrible weather.

ELIZABETH. Relentless.

HENRY. Still.

ELIZABETH. Yes.

He takes a nappy from the pile and dries his face.

HENRY. Where's Gabriel?

ELIZABETH. Asleep.

HENRY. Something happened on the train. (*Beat.*) It was crowded, stifling, standing room only, and I was completely lost in my own thoughts... when I realised that I had tucked my hand down the front of my trousers and was absent-mindedly pleasuring myself. (*Beat.*) I know.

ELIZABETH. You'll be arrested.

HENRY. At first I didn't think anyone saw me. I mean, nobody looks down there on the train.

ELIZABETH. The people with seats look down there. It's at their eye level.

HENRY. I know, but I thought nobody saw me. And then the train pulled into the platform and a woman approached and as she passed to get off she said, 'You should be ashamed. There are children on this train.' And I looked around and there were, several children, and I mean, I don't know if they were aware of what had happened but, Beth, I was appalled, I was so ashamed.

ELIZABETH. Well, it wasn't intentional.

HENRY. No.

ELIZABETH. You weren't deliberately trying to be offensive.

HENRY. No.

ELIZABETH. I mean, you're not one of those men who do it in public phone boxes and places like that, are you?

HENRY. Absolutely not.

ELIZABETH. Well, then... No wonder you forgot your umbrella.

HENRY. I'll look in on Gabriel.

ELIZABETH. Talk to me. I've been stuck indoors all day. I've been waiting for you to come home. You're late. I don't know where you are. I start thinking the worst.

HENRY. I was caught by the rain.

ELIZABETH. I need adult company, Henry. I'm going mad. I wasn't meant to be a mother. What were you thinking about, by the way, as you absent-mindedly pleasured yourself on the train?

HENRY. Well, the weather actually.

ELIZABETH. And you were aroused by this?

HENRY. No. At least not consciously. No, I was thinking about a hurricane.

ELIZABETH. Oh.

HENRY. In the year 1780. The deadliest hurricane in history tears the Caribbean apart. It bears the name of a Pope. Callixtus.

ELIZABETH. Credited with establishing the practice of absolution in the Christian Church for all repenting sinners.

HENRY. Well, yes. But Callixtus shows no mercy now. More than twenty-two thousand people are killed. The force of the rain strips the bark from the trees before it rips them from the earth. Not a single building is left standing on the island of Barbados. The same on St Kitts, St Lucia, St Vincent. Can you imagine, Beth, what it must be like to be at the centre of such a maelstrom?

ELIZABETH. I think it would be terrifying.

HENRY. Yes… The French naval fleet stationed off the island of Martinique was wiped out with the loss of four thousand sailors, delaying French intervention in the American War of Independence. If those four thousand men had have arrived on American soil when they were supposed to, the revolution would have triumphed three years before it did.

ELIZABETH. 'Man will never be free until the last king is strangled with the entrails of the last priest.'

HENRY. Diderot.

ELIZABETH. In 1780 as Callixtus wreaks havoc in the Caribbean on a biblical scale, in Paris Denis Diderot shakes the foundations of the Church with the publication of the final volume of his *Encyclopédie ou Dictionnaire raisonné des sciences, des arts et des métiers*.

HENRY. Your mind, Beth.

ELIZABETH. It is the culmination of twenty years of passion and labour to gather in a single collection all the great thinking of the times, all the new knowledge and revolutionary ideas that were challenging the rule of the aristocracy and the Church. It ushers in the birth of modern democratic thinking with its revolutionary beliefs of freedom of thought, religious tolerance, equality and justice for all. It changes the way human beings think about themselves. It is the dawn of the secular age and the foundation on which Marx built. It places science and art at the very centre of existence. Not God. But man as a rational and thinking being in control of his destiny. Responsible for his own actions. Able to think deeply and act decisively to change. For the better. To evolve. To save himself.

HENRY. The Enlightenment.

ELIZABETH. All this and the man still said of himself, 'I have been, and still am, angry at being mediocre.'

HENRY. What does that make the rest of us?

ELIZABETH. He is also the author of an essay titled 'Regrets on Parting with My Old Dressing Gown'. You might think the piece is whimsical but it's actually about man's propensity to consume more than he needs.

HENRY. He was ahead of his time.

ELIZABETH. Diderot was given a gift of a beautiful scarlet dressing gown and so pleased was he with this gift that he promptly threw out his old one. But as he wandered through his house he noticed that nothing else he owned matched the splendour of the new gown. The upholstery on his chairs was worn. The curtains in his study were faded. And the rest of his wardrobe just couldn't compare. And where previously, before possessing the splendid gown he had been content with his lot, for the first time in his life he felt a desire for new things. And so begins an endless process of acquisition and with each new acquisition, everything else seems old and in need of replacement. And so it goes. Desire for things driving the economy. Man's insatiable hunger for the new consuming the planet's resources at an exponential rate. It was a brilliant critique of capitalism before capitalism even existed. The question is, can we ever be happy with our old dressing gown again?

HENRY. What's the answer?

ELIZABETH. It remains to be seen... But I believe we can. (*Beat*.) Diderot also wrote several sentimental plays understood to be among the first works of the stage to treat the domestic life of ordinary people with any seriousness and compassion. Until Diderot, a woman at home folding nappies and thinking the worst whilst anxiously awaiting her husband's return from his day out in the world had no place on the stage. The stage was the province of kings.

HENRY. What is the worst... that you think while you wait for me?

ELIZABETH. That you have been with some other woman.

Beat.

HENRY. There is no other woman, Beth. Only inclement weather.

He exits.

ELIZABETH. Diderot also said, 'Only passions, great passions, can elevate the soul to great things.' But a woman without passion in her life, has nothing to do but wait. This last being said not by Diderot but by me.

It begins to rain.

ELIZABETH *appears to be standing in a park in the rain on a dark night.*

JOE *enters and* ELIZABETH *exits.*

And we are in

A Park

Adelaide 2013

It's raining. There is a hat on a park bench beneath a tree.

JOE *picks up his hat.*

JOE. Dear Son, I hope this letter finds you. I'm sending it to the last known address we have. I'm writing to let you know that your mother's not well. I'm not sure if you got my last letter. We received no reply. But she's getting worse, Gabriel, and I'm not sure what to do. She wants to see you. Please come. My love and best regards, Joe.

JOE *puts on his hat as*

The YOUNGER GABRIELLE *enters. She stares out over the waters of the Coorong. She holds an unlit cigarette in her hand.*

JOE *sees her or a memory of her.*

There you are.

GABRIELLE. Where?

JOE. By the sea. (*Beat.*) It's 1988. I'm twenty-four years old. I'm driving a Datsun 180B. I'm crossing the Hay Plain halfway between Sydney and Adelaide. I'm sitting on a hundred and ten k's, but I'm itching to go faster. Itching to get home. But the cops are up and down this stretch and I don't want to risk it. I'm heading back to my parents' farm on the Coorong. I tried the city. It didn't work. It's not for

me. Too fast. Too sharp. The Coorong's where I belong.
Dad's rapt. He'll be waiting at the gate pretending to fix a
fence. Mum will be in the kitchen. She's not so sure. She
doesn't think there's such a great future on the land. 'We've
messed it up,' she says, 'We've done the wrong thing.' But
nobody believes her. A visionary, my mum. A simple
woman but a visionary. So I'm sitting on a hundred and ten
and this Ford passes me, doing a hundred and forty at least.
Idiot. I say. Idiot. Hate that. Hate getting passed. You're
doing the right thing and somebody passes and it just makes
you feel like you're fifty years old or something. Then thirty
k's out of Narrandera I come around a bend and there she is,
the Ford, wrapped around a tree with steam coming out of
her bonnet.

I pull over. I get out. I move toward the car. I don't want to
look. There's blood on the windscreen. I bend down. The
driver's mincemeat. But there's a girl in there. She's
moaning. There's blood all over her face. 'Hey... hey, can
you hear me.' Her eyes open and she can see me, just for a
moment she sees me and then her eyes start to fade. I've
seen sheep die. I've seen dogs die. I've seen my grandma
die. I know that look. So I reach in and grab her hand.
'Hey... wake up. Stay with me,' and her eyes flick open
and I feel a faint pressure of her hand holding mine back.
'I've got you,' I say, 'I'm holding on. I've got you.'
Christ... where's the help? Where's the siren? Why aren't
there any fucking cars on this highway? And she's quiet.
Too quiet. And I squeeze her hand hard. I squeeze it so
hard. 'I'm not letting you go.' And I see her lips move,
she's trying to say something. I try and get as close as I
can, get right in there, into the twisted metal of it. 'What is
it? What are you trying to say?' And she says really quietly,
'You're hurting my hand.'

And I laughed. Probably not the right thing to do. I mean,
there's some bloke dead beside her, but it was the relief, you
know, I knew she was going to make it. So I ease up the
pressure a little but I keep holding on. 'What's your name?' I
say. 'Gabrielle.' What? 'Gabrielle. It's biblical,' she says.

And I know she's safe, this Gabrielle, but I'm holding on.

I'm still holding on.

GABRIEL LAW *enters and* JOE *exits*.

And we are on

A Beach

On the Coorong 1988

Night. Waves on the shore. A storm on the horizon.

GABRIEL. You smoke.

GABRIELLE. No, not really. I just wanted to hold one. My mother used to smoke. I used to think she looked so sophisticated and after... Well, I just felt like looking sophisticated.

GABRIEL. That was your first time, wasn't it?

GABRIELLE. Didn't know if I was meant to tell you. Thought I'd just let you find out. Told you I was different. Everybody else in this town got it out of the way before they left school. I used to think, no way, not me. I'm not giving it away. I'm holding on. For someone special. Not some bloke from around here. Before you know it I'm twenty-four and wishing I'd got rid of it when I was sixteen like all the other girls. So I'm standing at the window thinking I can't bear it any longer. I'm going crazy. I have to do something about this. And I turn around and there you are. And I think, he'll do. Not bad-looking, nice accent and at least he doesn't smell like fish and have sand between his toes and he won't tell his mates in the morning. So I used you. Sorry. But you can have a toasted sandwich on the house if you like.

GABRIEL. Well... thanks.

GABRIELLE. Don't think it means anything. Because it
doesn't. You can piss off in the morning. I got what I
wanted.

GABRIEL. Don't.

GABRIELLE. What?

GABRIEL. Sleep with me and then push me away.

GABRIELLE. Was that lightning? Did you see it?

GABRIEL. No.

GABRIELLE. Listen.

Sure enough, a rumble of thunder.

I hate nights like this. When I was a kid they would frighten
me. Still do. On nights like this, ships are lost at sea. I used
to wake up in the middle of the night. I thought I could hear
screaming. My father would tell me that it was just the gulls
calling for their mates in the wind. But I was sure there were
people drowning out there.

GABRIEL. Why did your parents kill themselves? (*Beat.*)
Sorry. That was an abrupt segue. You don't have to tell me.

GABRIELLE. I had a brother. He was taken.

GABRIEL. Taken?

GABRIELLE. They found his shoe on the beach… I don't want
to talk about this.

GABRIEL. Okay.

GABRIELLE. I can't talk about this. (*Beat.*) What's a segue?…
I mean, I've heard the word but I'm just not sure of its
meaning.

GABRIEL. It's a musical term. A movement, I guess, a
transition from one idea to another, only the two ideas aren't
necessarily related or their relationship is not obvious at first.
It's one of the things that make conversation interesting. It's
also a technique, if you like, to change the subject. Or to

prevent a person from talking about something you don't
want them to talk about.

GABRIELLE. What are you doing here, Gabriel?

GABRIEL. Like that. That was a segue.

GABRIELLE. On the Coorong in the middle of winter… a long
way from London.

GABRIEL *picks up a piece of driftwood, ancient and grey.*

GABRIEL. My father came here once. He sent me a postcard. It
had a picture of the Ninety Mile Beach. I wanted to see it for
myself. I even had thoughts of walking it. Until I saw what
ninety miles of beach actually looked like.

GABRIELLE. What did it say?

GABRIEL. 'Dear Gabriel, the Coorong is a dangerous place.
Caught between the land and the sea it belongs to neither. I
miss you. Dad.'

GABRIELLE. Is that all?

GABRIEL. Twenty-three words. I thought it might make sense
if I saw it for myself.

The YOUNGER ELIZABETH *enters and stands by the
window looking out.*

GABRIELLE. Does it?

GABRIEL. No.

GABRIELLE. Why didn't you ask him?

GABRIEL. I didn't get the chance. He left when I was seven.
Without a word. Which was another kind of segue all
together. But he sent me seven postcards… I found them in
my mother's sewing drawer when I was a child.

GABRIELLE. She kept them from you?

GABRIEL. Yes.

GABRIELLE. Why?

GABRIEL. There are some things she won't discuss. My father. The past. The fact that she drinks. These subjects are off-limits.

GABRIELLE. But it was cruel... to keep them from you.

GABRIEL. I guess she had her reasons.

GABRIELLE. You must hate her.

GABRIEL. I've tried to. But I can't. On the contrary.

GABRIELLE. What about your father... do you remember him?

GABRIEL. I wish I could say yes. I wish I could say that I remember the touch of his bristles on my face, or the scent of his aftershave, or the sound of his laughter in the morning. But I remember none of that. He's a mystery. What I remember is his absence and my mother's silence. All I have are his postcards. And they don't make much sense. They're full of wild predictions about the weather and the end of the world. In one he wrote that he had seen a vision of a fish falling from the sky and the earth being covered by water.

GABRIELLE. Was he mad?

GABRIEL. I don't know... Perhaps. The last postcard he wrote was sent from Ayers Rock. It has a picture of the rock with storm clouds gathering. It is bright red. Unbelievably red. With these great purple clouds ready to burst above it. 'Dear Son,' he wrote, 'in the desert, on a clear night, if you know where to look, you can see the planet Saturn. The word planet derives from the Greek and means wanderer. Saturn is named after the Roman god who devoured his own son. Forgive me. Your loving father, Henry Law. P.S. There's snow falling on the Rock tonight.'

GABRIELLE. It doesn't snow in the desert.

GABRIEL. No. And fish don't fall out of the sky. And fathers don't leave their children and mothers don't drown themselves in the sea. (*Beat.*) So that's what I'm doing here.

Trying to see what my father saw. Trying to think what he thought. Trying to understand why he went away. And then I pulled up at a roadhouse in the Coorong and saw this girl standing at the window who chose me, of all people, to help her get rid of something she no longer needed. And now I'm not sure. I'm not sure what it means. I didn't expect this.

GABRIELLE. We just fucked. (*Beat.*) That's all.

GABRIEL. Right.

GABRIELLE. Your father's right about the Coorong… You can be standing on solid ground then without even noticing, it turns to water beneath you. And if you don't move, you'll drown.

A flash of light on the horizon. A rumble of thunder.

The OLDER ELIZABETH *enters.*

GABRIEL. Here.

He gives her the piece of driftwood.

Keep this to remember your first time.

They proceed to exit.

ELIZABETH (OLDER). I might clear these plates.

GABRIELLE *continues to exit but* GABRIEL *remains as he did in the previous scene between him and his mother.*

The storm breaks around them.

Wind. Rain. The waves pounding on the shore.

And we are in

Elizabeth Law's Room

London 1988

GABRIEL. Let me help.

ELIZABETH. It's fine.

GABRIEL. I'll wash up, then.

ELIZABETH. I'll do it later. You don't want to miss your bus.

GABRIEL. But we've hardly spoken.

ELIZABETH. It's just that I'm a little tired. After my fall. I want to lie down.

GABRIEL. Is it because you want a drink? (*Beat.*) You've done very well, Mum. To get through lunch without one. Why don't you open a bottle? I don't mind. Where's your stash? I'll open it for you. Shall I have one with you? Or do you prefer to drink alone? (*Beat.*) I came here to tell you that I'm going away… to Australia. I'm not sure how long for. Must have been the newspaper clipping. Got my imagination going, but I'm keen to see this rock and I have such a yearning to stand under a different sky to the one I was born under.

She is silent.

Christ! (*Beat.*) I'll write… or phone or something, to let you know I'm okay. Is that alright? Will you want to know that?

He moves to her.

ELIZABETH. Don't.

GABRIEL. Mum… Please.

ELIZABETH. If you touch me now I will break.

HENRY *enters. His face is bloodied. His shirt is torn. He is wet from the storm.*

ELIZABETH (YOUNGER). Henry.

GABRIEL LAW *leaves but the* OLDER ELIZABETH *remains.*

And we are in

The Same Room

London 1965

ELIZABETH. Your face.

HENRY. There's been an accident.

ELIZABETH. What sort of accident?

HENRY. In the park... on my way home. Well, not an accident. I've been attacked.

ELIZABETH. Who by?

HENRY. Three men. They've taken my wallet.

ELIZABETH. Let me...

She attempts to clean the blood from his face.

HENRY. Where's Gabriel?

ELIZABETH. He's in the bath.

HENRY. Will he be alright?

ELIZABETH. He's five years old. He'll be fine. Have you spoken to the police?

HENRY. No.

ELIZABETH. I'll call them.

HENRY. No. I'd rather not involve them... They might have followed me. They might know where we live.

ELIZABETH. All the more reason to call the police.

HENRY. We don't want any trouble.

ELIZABETH. I don't understand.

HENRY. I'm alright.

ELIZABETH. That's clearly not true.

HENRY. Why did they pick me, Beth? What's wrong with me?

ELIZABETH. Nothing. There's nothing wrong with you.

HENRY. We could go away.

ELIZABETH. What?

HENRY. We could leave London... take Gabriel and start again.

ELIZABETH. Leave... where would we go?

HENRY. I don't know... Australia.

ELIZABETH. What?

HENRY. Why not?

ELIZABETH. We can't leave just because some men beat you in the park.

HENRY. I've been thinking about this.

ELIZABETH. But Australia... it's so far.

HENRY. Yes.

ELIZABETH. It's the end of the world.

HENRY. I have such a yearning... to be more than I am.

ELIZABETH. But you're everything. To me you're everything. What more could you be?

The OLDER ELIZABETH *takes a bottle of wine and a glass from her hiding place and pours herself a glass.*

HENRY. I couldn't bear to lose Gabriel.

ELIZABETH. You won't... What are you talking about?

HENRY. Sometimes I think I can see the future.

ELIZABETH. Don't say that… You don't have the right to see the future.

The YOUNGER ELIZABETH *exits as the* OLDER ELIZABETH *slowly raises her glass to her lips.*

HENRY *exits.*

And we are in

A Graveyard

On the Coorong 1988

The YOUNGER GABRIELLE *stands before three headstones.*

The OLDER GABRIELLE *enters and stands at a distance watching her. She wears her nightgown and is lost somewhere in her memory.*

GABRIELLE (OLDER). 'Georgia York. Née Bray. 1940 to 1971. Beloved wife and mother.' She wore a frock well and looked good when she smoked a cigarette. 'Peter James York. 1939 to 1985.' He had a slight stoop and a crooked smile. And never thought he was good enough. 'Glen Peter York. 1960 to 1968.' He built sandcastles on the beach.

GABRIEL LAW *enters.*

GABRIEL. There you are.

GABRIELLE (YOUNGER). You're going?

GABRIEL. Yes. I'm all packed.

GABRIELLE. Where will you go?

GABRIEL. To the Centre… Isn't that what you call it?

GABRIELLE. It's another country out there.

GABRIEL *joins her at the graves. He reads the headstones.*

GABRIEL. Your brother was only eight.

GABRIELLE. Seven. He hadn't turned eight yet.

GABRIEL. We were born in the same year. (*Beat.*) I'm not him.

GABRIELLE. I know that.

GABRIEL. It's a coincidence.

GABRIELLE. I know.

Beat.

GABRIEL. Were you close?

GABRIELLE. There's a photo of us. On the beach. He's holding my hand. But I don't remember him. It's like your father. I remember him because he wasn't there.

GABRIEL. What happened to him, Gabrielle?

GABRIELLE. They found his shoe on the beach... they thought the sea had taken him. That's what they hoped. Then a fisherman found his clothes in the sandhills. Shorts. T-shirt. Underpants. Eventually they found his bones. They'd been uncovered by the wind. Buried in a shallow grave.

GABRIEL. Are you saying he was murdered?

GABRIELLE. That's what sent my mother over the edge. What had been done to him. (*Beat.*) At least Dad had the decency to wait until I finished school and had a job. He was dead anyway, of course. He died the day Glen was taken and then he died again the day Mum went. But he saw me through, more or less. Kind of half there. But Mum couldn't wait. She didn't think the child that was left was worth it. (*Beat.*) They're cruel, aren't they, parents? They're so fucking cruel.

They are silent.

I wasn't sure I could trust you. I was pretending to be strong, then, last night on the beach I realised I'm not the only one.

GABRIEL. Come with me.

GABRIELLE. Don't. I'm not just some girl you meet in a roadhouse who you hook up with for a couple of months before you piss off back to London. I'm not that girl.

GABRIEL. I know that... and I'm not that boy.

GABRIELLE. What's the good of it, you and me? We're too different.

GABRIEL. We have the same name... (*Beat.*) Is this going to be your life? Working in a roadhouse and getting the occasional shag from a passing tourist.

She stares at the headstones.

Let the dead take care of the dead.

GABRIELLE. I can't.

Beat.

GABRIEL. The car's parked over there... I'll turn on the radio and listen to one song. When the song finishes, I'll leave.

He exits.

GABRIELLE (OLDER). You're twenty-four years old. You work in a roadhouse in the Coorong. You play netball on Tuesday nights and clean the bird shit from the headstones of the graves of your family on Sunday. You know that if you don't leave here soon you will marry a farmer from Salt Creek. He will be a good man who works hard and likes a beer. He will love you and you will make his life hell because that's not the life you want. You will go mad in that life. But you don't know what other life there is. Then this man, this stranger walks into the roadhouse, in the middle of winter, all the way from London, and orders a toasted sandwich with no ham, and talks about things that they don't talk about in the Coorong. He says let the dead take care of the dead. And now he's sitting in the car with the engine running listening to a song on the radio. And you know the song. You know it well. You know the last verse has just begun, you know the words, you could sing them, and when it's done you know you'll hear the tyres on the gravel and he will be gone and you may as well start looking for your wedding dress. You want to go, you want to run, you want to leave these ghosts behind but you're scared. In your stomach, in the pit of your stomach you know there is something wrong and that you should not get in that car.

GABRIELLE (YOUNGER). Wait, Gabriel.

She exits.

GABRIELLE (OLDER). Let the dead take care of the dead.

JOE *stands at the door in his pyjamas.*

JOE. Who are you talking to, love?

And we are in

Joe and Gabrielle's Room

Adelaide 2013

GABRIELLE. Myself.

JOE. Come back to bed. (*Beat.*) Gaby?

GABRIELLE. My name's not Gaby. It's Gabrielle. It's biblical… (*She looks at him.*) Who are you again?

JOE. It's Joe, love… your husband.

GABRIELLE. Joe?

JOE. Yes, love?

GABRIELLE. I want you to go. (*Beat.*) Did you hear what I said… I want you to go.

JOE. You don't mean that.

GABRIELLE. Yes I do.

JOE. You're not yourself.

GABRIELLE. Then who am I?... Who am I, Joe?... Who the fuck am I?

JOE. Don't speak like that.

GABRIELLE. Fuck you... who am I?

JOE. Your name is Gabrielle York. And I'm Joe Ryan. You're my wife. And this is our flat. This is where we live.

GABRIELLE. I don't understand.

JOE. You're upset, that's all.

GABRIELLE. I didn't want this.

JOE *moves to comfort her.*

Don't.

He stops. He can't bear seeing this.

I want you to go.

JOE. But it's raining.

GABRIELLE. Then take your hat and your umbrella and your raincoat and go.

JOE. Please, Gabrielle... don't do this.

GABRIELLE. Get out... Get the fuck out.

JOE *takes his hat and umbrella and raincoat and leaves the apartment.*

Everything has turned to shit.

A carpet of stars appears above her. In the distance she sees the light of a campfire. She exits.

And we are at

The Campsite

Uluru 1988

GABRIEL *and* GABRIELLE *sit by a fire beneath the carpet of stars.* GABRIEL *is writing.* GABRIELLE *watches the flames.*

The OLDER ELIZABETH *remains at the table with her bottle of wine.*

The YOUNGER ELIZABETH *enters. She pours a glass of wine and sits at the table opposite her older self. Simultaneously they raise their glasses to their lips and sip their wine.*

The OLDER ELIZABETH *unfolds a letter and begins to read.*

ELIZABETH (OLDER). 'Dear Mum, I'm writing this from Ayers Rock or Uluru as it is now called. We have been driving for three days.

> GABRIELLE *looks up and watches* GABRIEL.

I'm sitting beneath a carpet of stars. It is more beautiful than I ever imagined. This southern sky. It is just before dawn and I am waiting for the Rock to appear.

> GABRIELLE *rises and moves away.* GABRIEL *looks up and watches her.*

I wanted to tell you that I have met someone. Her name is Gabrielle York. And although we have only known each other for a short time I feel as though she is somebody who I can love and who might love me in return.

> GABRIEL *rises and joins* GABRIELLE.

I'm sorry that we parted on such bad terms, but isn't it funny, how over the years we have found a way not to talk about the difficult things. There has been so much that I have wanted to know. And so much that you have been unable to tell me. My father remains a mystery to me. As in many ways you do. But I just wanted to tell you, Mum, that I am happy. Your son, Gabriel.'

GABRIELLE. Why did your father ask for your forgiveness?

Beat.

GABRIEL. He went away... he left me.

GABRIELLE. But why?

A wind picks up as it does in the desert just before dawn...

GABRIEL. It's dawn, Gabrielle... look...

... and light slowly falls upon Uluru as it seems to rise up from the darkness before them. They stand mesmerised before its towering ochre form and graceful curves.

It is a sight to behold.

GABRIELLE. I don't want you to go up there.

GABRIEL. What?

GABRIELLE. Don't climb it.

GABRIEL. Don't ask me that.

GABRIELLE. I am asking you.

GABRIEL. I've come a long way to do this, Gabrielle.

GABRIELLE. I don't care how far you've come.

GABRIEL. It's something I have to do.

GABRIELLE. Why?

GABRIEL. Because he went up there. He climbed that rock. A fair-skinned Englishman... and he never came back.

GABRIELLE. Let the dead take care of the dead.

GABRIEL. Are you making me choose?

GABRIELLE. Yes.

GABRIEL. Then I choose him.

Beat. GABRIELLE *turns to exit.*

Gabrielle…

She hesitates… then exits.

GABRIEL *looks toward the Rock. He moves toward it as…*

Both ELIZABETHS *slowly raise their glasses to their lips and sip their wine as*

GABRIEL *disappears into the darkness and*

HENRY *enters.*

ELIZABETH (YOUNGER). There you are.

And we are in

Henry and Elizabeth's Room

London 1968

HENRY *shakes the water from his umbrella and hangs it on a hook. He removes his raincoat and hangs it beside the umbrella.*

HENRY. Wine?… That's not like you.

ELIZABETH. I bought a bottle at the off-licence. An Australian claret. It's a little heavy.

HENRY. Robust, I think they call it. Like the people. Apparently. (*He moves to the window and looks down to the street below.*) Have you heard? The Soviets have invaded Czechoslovakia.

ELIZABETH. No. I missed that.

HENRY. Have you done something?

ELIZABETH. Yes. I've painted the walls.

HENRY. When?

ELIZABETH. As the tanks were rolling into Prague. Apparently. Do you like the colour?

HENRY. Well, it's white.

ELIZABETH. Off-white. Pure white is too stark. Like a hospital.

HENRY. Perhaps you could have chosen something bolder?

ELIZABETH. Bolder.

HENRY. Yes, like a colour.

ELIZABETH. Like red?

HENRY. Yes, why not?

ELIZABETH. Because it's the colour of blood.

She throws her glass of wine into his face.

And wine. (*Beat.*) Isn't it sad, Henry? Isn't it sad that we have drifted so far from one another that we have nothing left to talk about other than the colour of the walls?

HENRY. Beth…

ELIZABETH. We've drifted so far that I can hardly see you. You're just a shadow. An outline. A vapour of a man.

HENRY. What's happened?

ELIZABETH. Two policemen came here. To our flat.

HENRY. Where's Gabriel?

ELIZABETH. They wanted to question me about an incident in the park involving you apparently… and a seven-year-old boy.

HENRY. There was a misunderstanding.

ELIZABETH. There has been an accusation that you touched him inappropriately whilst the mother was waiting outside.

HENRY. The boy was having difficulty.

ELIZABETH. I don't understand… what difficulty does a seven-year-old boy have in a public lavatory?

HENRY. He wet himself. I was helping. He misunderstood and became upset. He must have said something to his mother. Beth, don't let your mind run away.

ELIZABETH. Well, that's what I thought. I thought my mind is running away. Clearly, I was going mad. And that's what I told them, of course. There's been some misunderstanding. I know my husband. He doesn't interfere with children. He has a son of his own. He's a father.

HENRY. Where is Gabriel?

ELIZABETH. Nevertheless, they said, they still want to speak to you.

HENRY. I haven't done anything. This is not right.

ELIZABETH. That's what I said. I said this is not right. How dare you accuse my husband of such a thing. Against nature. And I sent them on their way, Henry. I showed them the door. I could not have been more indignant. And when they were gone and I was alone, it felt to me as if the world had been turned upside down. And I looked around and saw just how dirty our room was. Filthy, in fact. In the corners and on the window sills and the ceilings. Layers of dust and dirt and grime and dead insects. Years of neglect, Henry. How did we let it come to this? And so I began to clean it. A bucket of hot water and soap suds. I washed the walls, the ceilings, even the light fittings were scrubbed. I washed the door handles and the light switches and the dark corners behind the furniture. I scrubbed the table and the floor and polished the windows. I dusted the books and the lampshade and even took to the grouting between the tiles with a toothbrush. And when I finished I looked around and it looked exactly the same. So I found an old tin of leftover paint in the cupboard. And as the tanks rolled into Prague I painted. And I painted. And I painted. Then I hung the pictures back on the walls. And put the books back on the bookshelves and moved the furniture back into position and it was when I was moving the wardrobe that it tilted slightly and something slipped from the top... and landed at my feet. (*Beat.*) A leather satchel. Quite old. Quite worn. Good-quality leather. Something you have had since you were a child. Given to you by an uncle, you once said. And inside there is a collection of photographs of young children, boys mainly, naked, some involved in sexual acts with adults. Some of them clearly distressed. Clearly frightened. And among the photographs. Among the photographs, Henry, are pictures of our own son.

Silence.

Have you touched him?

HENRY. No.

ELIZABETH. Have you?

HENRY. No.

ELIZABETH. Have you?

HENRY. No… But I'm frightened, Beth… that I will. (*Beat.*) What kind of man am I? What in nature makes a man like me? (*Beat.*) I didn't choose this.

ELIZABETH. No, I don't imagine one would… choose it.

HENRY. Please.

ELIZABETH. You'll have to go, of course.

HENRY. Of course, I'll find a room somewhere.

ELIZABETH. No, Henry, no… I want you gone… out of the country… out of our lives… out of existence. (*Beat.*) If you refuse, of course, I will hand that satchel to those two policemen. They've left their card.

HENRY. Where will I go?

ELIZABETH. Australia would be far enough. You're not the first Englishman to be sent there in shame.

HENRY. And Gabriel?

ELIZABETH. Well, exactly.

HENRY. I want to see him.

ELIZABETH. No.

HENRY. Let me speak to him.

ELIZABETH. No.

HENRY. Beth... please... if you have any feelings for me then let me say goodbye to my son.

ELIZABETH. I have feelings for you, Henry. That's why I'm sending you away and not turning you over to the authorities. I love you. Strangely, as abhorrent as this is, that hasn't changed. I imagine it will in time and whatever I feel for you will turn, but now... I still love you. But you're a thief. Instead of a loaf of bread you have stolen the future. And I will remove every trace of you from Gabriel's life. And every time the boy asks about you, about his father, and inevitably he will, I will remain silent. It will be as if you never existed.

ELIZABETH *walks slowly away and with each step she grows a little smaller until she is just nothing at all.*

A hot dry wind blows across the desert.

The OLDER ELIZABETH *exits.*

And we are

On Top of Uluru

1970 1988

A windswept and bleak terrain. It is night.

HENRY *looks across the darkness of the landscape below.*

HENRY. Dear Gabriel, it is a six-week journey from England to Australia by sea. We encountered many storms and saw many whales along the way. Your loving father. Dear Gabriel, the city of Perth is among the prettiest cities I have seen. I watch the children playing on Cottesloe Beach and think of you. Your loving father. Dear Gabriel, on the Nullarbor the desert holds back the sea. The waves smash against the cliffs with relentless power. And with each onslaught the earth gives way another inch. I miss you. Dear Gabriel, the Coorong is a dangerous place. Caught between the land and the sea it belongs to neither. I miss you. Dear Gabriel, in the Australian desert the earth is the colour of blood. I miss you. Dear Son, in the desert I saw a vision of the end. A fish fell from the sky and the earth became sea. I miss you. Dear Son, in the desert, on a clear night, if you know where to look, you can see the planet Saturn. The word planet derives from the Greek and means wanderer. Saturn is named after the Roman god who devoured his own son. Forgive me. Your loving father, Henry Law.

GABRIEL LAW *enters… and moves toward the edge of the fall.*

GABRIEL. There's no light here. No moon. No stars. No light. Just darkness.

HENRY. If you look across the desert, the earth takes on the appearance of the sea. You think you're standing upon a rock that rises from solid ground only to discover that you're standing on an island in the middle of the ocean. And you don't know if you're looking back into the past or into the future.

GABRIELLE *enters. She sees* GABRIEL *in the darkness.*

Water covered this earth and water will cover it again and the days that man walked here will prove just a moment in time. And all our knowledge, all our science, all our money and all our will won't stop it. It's too late. All our magnificent endeavour will come to nothing. And time will go on without us and it will be as if we were never here. (*Beat.*) Come with me, Gabriel.

GABRIEL. Dad?

GABRIELLE. Gabriel?

HENRY. Come with me.

GABRIELLE. Step back from the edge.

HENRY. Please, Son, I'm so lonely.

GABRIELLE. Look… it's snowing.

And it is.

He looks at GABRIELLE, *illuminated by the snow. And then back to* HENRY.

HENRY. Forgive me.

Then HENRY *falls into darkness.*

GABRIELLE. Come back from the edge.

GABRIEL walks back toward GABRIELLE *as the snow lights the way.*

It's beautiful, Gabriel… it's so beautiful.

They stand on Uluru in the falling snow.

A Park

Adelaide 2013

Snowfall.

JOE *sits on a park bench wearing his raincoat over his pyjamas. He looks up at the falling snow as the* OLDER GABRIELLE *enters wearing her raincoat over her nightgown.*

GABRIELLE. There you are.

JOE. Where?

GABRIELLE. Sitting on a park bench… in the snow.

JOE. Am I? Thought I was dancing the waltz at a Viennese ball.

She sits down beside him.

The weather is turning against us, Gabrielle. It should not be snowing in Adelaide.

GABRIELLE. But it's beautiful, Joe... it's so beautiful. (*Beat.*) Have I hurt you?

JOE. No.

GABRIELLE. Have I made your life hell?

JOE. No.

GABRIELLE. You're a liar.

JOE. Being turfed out of the flat on an ugly night in the middle of winter tests the patience a little. But there's not one day I regret being with you. Not one. And don't you say a word to contradict that because I know what I feel. And I know that you can't say the same. I stole you. I know that. Got you at a weak moment. You needed someone. And I made sure it was me. One thing you've got to give me credit for though is my patience. I have waited twenty-five years for you to love me.

GABRIELLE. And now I'm losing my mind. (*Beat.*) I'm angry, Joe. Always have been.

JOE. I know.

GABRIELLE. No you don't. The only time I ever saw you angry was when you hit your thumb with a hammer. And you didn't even swear.

JOE. No, well, I don't like language. It was just the way I was brought up. Can't help that.

GABRIELLE. Sometimes I wish you would just scream.

JOE. I don't know what that would achieve.

GABRIELLE. It would tell the world that you're in pain.

JOE. I'm not sure the world would care. (*Beat.*) I wish I'd never stopped the car... Yeah, there you go. I've said it. I wish I just put my foot down and let you bleed to death. With him. I would have made it back to the Coorong and met some half-decent girl who would have loved me.

GABRIELLE. I have loved you.

JOE. Not the way I have loved you.

GABRIELLE. You love too much.

JOE. Don't say that to me. Because there is some woman in Salt Creek who would have known how to be loved by me. And don't tell me you're angry. Who do you think you've been angry at for twenty-five years? Loyal old Joe, that's who. Like a dog, that's what I am. And why? Because I saved you. Because I never measured up to something I never even understood. But don't you dare measure me against him. Twenty-five years it's been. Against what? A couple of weeks? If that? I have raised his son and lived with his ashes in the cupboard for twenty-five years. And you're wrong. I have been angry every day of my life since I met you. I have been angry at myself for being unable to make you happy. (*Beat.*) And I'm not the only one who tried.

GABRIELLE. Don't.

JOE. You made my life hell, but what's worse... you did the same to your son.

GABRIELLE. No.

JOE. It's true, Gabrielle. In the end the boy couldn't wait to leave.

GABRIELLE. Did he call?

JOE. No.

GABRIELLE. I thought that maybe...

JOE. No. He hasn't called for seven years.

Beat.

GABRIELLE. They're cruel, aren't they? Children. They're so fucking cruel.

Silence.

I've had enough.

JOE. Come on, then.

GABRIELLE. No, love. I want you to let me go. (*Beat*.) There are pills in my bedside drawer.

JOE. No.

GABRIELLE. Help me do this.

JOE. I can't.

GABRIELLE. I'm going anyway. A month. Two. Six at the most. And I'm gone. I won't know who you are. I won't know who Gabriel is. I won't even know who I am.

JOE. You're asking too much.

GABRIELLE. I always have. (*Beat*.) It's only life. And I've had a miserable one and I've had enough of it. This goes way back, Joe, way before you. It was your bad luck that you stopped the car but you did and that's your lot, but mine goes way back... to a little kid playing on the beach... and the bastard that took him. That's all. Not your fault. Not my fault. But I've had enough now, Joe. I have seen death every way and I'm not afraid of it. (*Beat*.) Take me home now... Make love to me. You big gorgeous thing.

JOE. Gorgeous?

GABRIELLE. Yeah... I've always thought so. You've been alright in the sack too. At first it was like you were shearing and I was the sheep, but you got better, Joe. Over the years you got better. You learnt such tenderness. But it's been a while... can't remember the last time.

JOE. It was 2010. Three years ago.

GABRIELLE. Christ!... I want clean sheets and candles and music and when we're finished I want you to let me go.

JOE. What am I going to do without you?

GABRIELLE. I don't know, love. Go back to the Coorong. Find that woman in Salt Creek. She's probably still there...

They proceed to exit as

GABRIEL LAW *and the* YOUNGER GABRIELLE *appear.*

The OLDER GABRIELLE *hesitates and looks back at them.*

GABRIELLE (YOUNGER). I love being in a car at night.

And we are in

A Car

On the Hay Plain 1988

Headlights pick out the road ahead as the car moves down the highway at a hundred and forty kilometres per hour. But inside the car, all is still. GABRIELLE *stares into the light cast on the road ahead.*

GABRIEL. Why?

GABRIELLE. Because you can only see so far ahead and that's enough, for now.

GABRIEL. I love you.

GABRIELLE. Don't say that.

GABRIEL. Why not?

GABRIELLE. Because it has to mean something. For you and me of all people it has to mean something. Because every time somebody leaves us it's going to be like your father or my parents all over again. That's how hard it's going to be. So if you tell me you love me, that's it. It's for ever. If you don't mean that then I don't want to hear it.

GABRIEL. I love you... I have never been more certain about what I feel... I love you, Gabrielle York.

GABRIELLE (OLDER). You're twenty-four years old. You're staring down the highway. It's all open road ahead. The Coorong is already starting to feel like just a memory.

There's something stirring in your belly. You think it's
nerves… you think it's happiness because there's this bloke
sitting at the wheel beside you, this English bloke who came
out of nowhere and saved you from something big and he's
saying he loves you and you think you could love him.
Maybe. Yeah, you could love him. And for a moment you
can see a life worth living. But you don't trust it. You don't
trust this. You know you weren't meant to be happy. And
there's something on your mind, something eating at you,
one thing that you know could ruin it. You could say nothing.
For his sake you could let it be. For your sake you could let
it go. But you have to know.

GABRIELLE (YOUNGER). What year was your father in the
Coorong?

GABRIEL. 1968.

GABRIELLE. The year my brother was taken.

GABRIEL *looks across at her as the weight of this tragic
possibility dawns on him.*

The road, Gabriel.

The OLDER GABRIELLE *turns away and leaves.*

Watch the road.

We are in

Four Rooms

1968 1988 1988 2013

Each superimposed upon the other. A telephone is ringing.

The OLDER ELIZABETH *sits at the table with a bottle of wine
and a glass before her as the* YOUNGER ELIZABETH *enters
and proceeds to set the table for two.*

The OLDER ELIZABETH *rises and moves forward to answer the phone.*

ELIZABETH (OLDER). Yes?

Silence. The YOUNGER ELIZABETH *hesitates, plate in hand.*

Who is this?

The YOUNGER GABRIELLE *enters.*

GABRIELLE. My name is Gabrielle York... I'm calling from Australia... There's been an accident... I'm sorry... Gabriel has been killed.

A silence between them as she contains the dam of emotion threatening to break.

Are you there?

ELIZABETH. Yes, I'm here... I'm still here.

GABRIELLE. They said he didn't suffer.

ELIZABETH. Did they?... How would they know? (*Beat.*) He mentioned you in a letter. He said that he thought you were someone he could love and who might love him in return. Did you love him or was it just wishful thinking on his behalf?

GABRIELLE. Yes... I think I loved him.

ELIZABETH. I'm not sure it's something one thinks. It's something one knows, surely.

GABRIELLE. I loved him.

ELIZABETH. Did he know that he was loved?

GABRIELLE. I don't know... I never told him.

ELIZABETH. Nor did I... I often meant to but these things, these moments, they slip away. It's terrible but you reach a time in your life when you realise that you have very little to say to your children. Of course having nothing to say is just another way of having so much to say that you dare not begin. (*Beat*.) Could I ask you to arrange a funeral? I don't think I could go to Australia. It's such a long way.

GABRIELLE. Yes, I can do that… I know how to do that.

ELIZABETH. I'll send money, of course. I have some put away. I think a cremation would be best.

GABRIELLE. If that's what you want… I can send the ashes to England.

ELIZABETH. I think it's better if they stayed there, don't you? I'm sure you will find the right thing to do with them.

The OLDER GABRIELLE *enters carrying the urn containing Gabriel's ashes. Through the following she places it on the table and takes a bowl of soup and takes a place at the table.*

GABRIELLE. I'm pregnant.

Beat.

ELIZABETH. Would you like me to send money for you to take care of that as well?… I'm not meaning to be cruel.

GABRIELLE. Aren't you?

ELIZABETH. How old are you?

GABRIELLE. Twenty-four.

ELIZABETH. Think carefully before you make your decision. You're very young and bringing up a child on your own is a heavy price to pay for a brief affair with a melancholic English boy. The decision is yours, of course.

GABRIELLE. I know that… I wasn't asking your permission. If it's a boy I will call him Gabriel.

ELIZABETH. Do you think that's wise? It would be tragic if every time you said your son's name you were reminded of what you had lost.

GABRIELLE. I asked him once if he hated you… He said that he tried. But he couldn't. On the contrary, he said… I knew

then how strong he was… to love someone who was
incapable of being loved.

ELIZABETH. Don't presume so much.

GABRIELLE. I'm not talking about you. (*Beat.*) I have to ask
you about Gabriel's father. (*Beat.*) I had a brother. He was
taken from the beach by a stranger in 1968.

Silence.

Please.

Silence.

Talk to me.

ELIZABETH. Did Gabriel know?

GABRIELLE. Yes. It was the last thing he knew.

   ELIZABETH *slowly disconnects the line.*

GABRIELLE. Wait… Don't go… Don't leave me.

   Beat. ELIZABETH *walks away from the phone call.*

ELIZABETH. I had a fall. In the street. Every woman's worst
fear, of a certain age. A turning point into decline. But when
I fell I thought I heard a man scream. That's what made me
stumble, I'm sure. A scream. And for a moment, I thought it
was the future screaming at me. (*Beat.*) Sometimes I feel
like I'm getting smaller. Sometimes I feel like I'm just
nothing at all. But then I catch a glimpse of myself in the
mirror and I see that I am still here. (*Beat.*) I'm still here.
(*Beat.*) I'm still here.

   The OLDER GABRIELLE *takes the ashes and slowly pours
   them into the soup. She stirs them into the liquid and then,
   slowly and deliberately, she proceeds to eat it.*

   *As the other three women place their hands on their bellies
   and hold their stillness until* GABRIELLE *has completed
   her meal.*

JOE *enters.*

JOE. It's ready, love… bed made, candles lit, music playing.

GABRIELLE looks up from her bowl… no longer with him.

GABRIELLE. Who are you again?

Beat. JOE walks slowly away and stands before the audience.

JOE. Dear Gabriel… I hope this letter finds you. I'm writing to let you know that your mother has passed away. She died peacefully in her sleep. Her last thoughts were of you. If you should choose to return, you will find some things she wanted you to have in a small suitcase. My love. Joe.

JOE stands in silence before us. Then he opens his mouth and screams.

Let us finish with

Gabriel York's Room

Alice Springs 2039

GABRIEL YORK sits at the table set for two. He wears no socks. He looks up at the sound of a knock at the door.

GABRIEL. Andrew?

He rises from the table as his son, ANDREW PRICE, enters. He carries a wrapped box.

A moment just to take the other in, then ANDREW kisses his father on the cheek. An awkward moment but a striking one.

Well… look at this.

ANDREW. I'm sorry I'm late. I was held up by the rain.

GABRIEL. Terrible weather. In Alice Springs! Still, there are people drowning in Bangladesh, so we shouldn't complain.

ANDREW. I know. It's terrible.

GABRIEL. What?

ANDREW. What's happening in Bangladesh. (*Beat.*) You haven't heard the news.

GABRIEL. No, I don't follow it.

ANDREW. There's unprecedented flooding. Large parts of the country are underwater. The death toll is near half a million and rising. And it's not just Bangladesh. Severe flooding is threatening low-lying areas of Northern Europe and Southern America... There are people out there saying this is the end.

GABRIEL. The end of what?

ANDREW. The end of the world... That's why I wanted to see you.

GABRIEL. I imagine it's been quite an ordeal to get here.

ANDREW. Yeah... in so many ways.

Beat.

GABRIEL. You're a fine-looking young man. Must have got that from your mother.

ANDREW. I have your eyes apparently.

GABRIEL. Yes, you do... I remember that. You had my eyes. And you still do. But your mother has done a good job, I can see that.

ANDREW. It wasn't easy for her.

GABRIEL. No. (*Beat.*) Are you hungry? Lunch is almost ready... It's fish... I hope you eat it.

ANDREW. What, fish from the sea?

GABRIEL. Well... strangely, yes.

ANDREW. I don't think I've eaten that.

GABRIEL. They say it's very good for you. Good for the brain. Or something.

ANDREW. You shouldn't have gone to that much trouble.

GABRIEL. It was less trouble than you think… If it is the end of the world then I can't think of anything I'd rather eat than fish, can you?

ANDREW. No.

GABRIEL. Or anyone I'd rather share it with.

Beat.

ANDREW. I brought you something.

He hands GABRIEL *the gift.*

I didn't know what to get you… I asked in the shop. I said, what do you give a father who you haven't seen since you were seven years old? Then I saw this.

Beat. Then GABRIEL *pulls out a splendid new scarlet dressing gown.*

Do you like it?

GABRIEL. It's beautiful.

ANDREW. Put it on.

GABRIEL *puts the dressing gown over his suit.*

Yeah… that's it. That's how I remember you…

GABRIEL. I used to have an old one… when I…

ANDREW. Yeah. You used to wear it around the house. (*Beat.*) It suits you.

GABRIEL. Do you think so? I'm not sure it suits the flat, though.

ANDREW. Why?

GABRIEL. It makes everything else look a little old.

ANDREW. Maybe.

GABRIEL. Perhaps I'll get some new furniture to match it. But then again, if it is the end of the world…

ANDREW. Exactly.

GABRIEL. Besides… I'm happy with what I have. (*Beat.*) How long will you stay?

ANDREW. I'm not sure.

GABRIEL. You're welcome to stay here, if you need a place.

ANDREW. I wouldn't want to put you to any trouble.

GABRIEL. It's no trouble. And to tell you the truth I'd like the company. And it would give us some time. Because there's such a lot to say, Andrew… such a lot to explain.

ANDREW. Like why you left when I was so young?

GABRIEL. Are you angry?

ANDREW. Not any more… I don't think I could be here if I was still angry. I don't even know if anger is what I felt. I think I just felt bewildered. Like why bother being there in the first place, leaving me with just enough memories to know what I had lost.

GABRIEL. What do you remember?

ANDREW. The touch of your bristles on my face, and the smell of your aftershave, and the sound of your laughter in the morning.

GABRIEL. I laughed?

ANDREW. Yeah, you laughed.

GABRIEL. What at?

ANDREW. At me. I made you laugh. You would see me and your face would light up and you would laugh.

GABRIEL. I remember.

ANDREW. Then why did you leave?

Beat.

GABRIEL. There's something I want to show you.

GABRIEL *exits.* ANDREW *moves to the window and looks down into the street below as*

The OLDER *and the* YOUNGER ELIZABETH, *the* OLDER *and the* YOUNGER GABRIELLE, GABRIEL LAW *and* JOE *enter. Each takes a plate from a pile and takes a place at the table.* ANDREW *turns from the window and takes his place at the end of the table as*

GABRIEL YORK *enters with the old suitcase.*

GABRIEL. I wanted to give you something. And I don't have much money –

ANDREW. I don't want –

GABRIEL. I know… but I wanted to give you something all the same. You see, I have spent my life running from my past and yet I have carried fragments of it around in this old suitcase… And I don't know if these few things will make much sense to you… they hardly make sense to me but it's all I have to give you.

He opens the suitcase and, with each object he removes, he passes it to the ancestor who sits in the place next to him who in turn passes it on down the table until it reaches ANDREW *at the other end.* ANDREW *takes each object with reverence and curiosity.*

GABRIEL *takes out a piece of driftwood.*

My mother kept this on her dressing table. I caught her once standing in her room holding it. She had tears in her eyes. I never asked her why it made her cry… I wish I had.

A boy's shoe. I don't know who it belonged to. I don't think it was one of mine… She kept it in her drawer wrapped in tissue paper.

And this is the urn that contained my father's ashes. I know they were in there because I looked when I was a child. I wasn't meant to but children will always look in the places where they're not allowed. It's empty now. I don't know what happened to the ashes.

This is a book that arrived from England when I was twelve years old. It is written in French and is some kind of encyclopedia. It was sent by my English grandmother with a note tucked inside. 'Read this and you might change the world. And if you can't read French, then learn it.' There was no return address. And I never heard from her again. I never got round to learning the language so it remains unread and the world remains unchanged.

This is my stepfather's hat. His name was Joe Ryan. He was a good man and I loved him very much. He disappeared after my mother's death.

And these are the letters he sent me telling me that she was dying... I am ashamed to say that I never replied to them.

ANDREW. Why not?

GABRIEL. You reach a moment in your life when you realise that you have nothing to say to your parents. I reached that moment with my own mother when I was seventeen years old. It wasn't until years later that I realised that having nothing to say is just another way of having so much to say that you dare not begin... And by then, it was too late. She was gone... I wish I had more courage, Andrew. I wish I had your courage. (*Beat.*) These are my father's postcards. His name was Gabriel Law and they were sent to him by his father, Henry Law. I never met my father. He died in a car accident before I was born. But I know that he met my mother in a roadhouse on the Coorong. And that she loved him deeply. So deeply that she could barely mention his name. Which was unfortunate.

The last postcard Henry wrote was sent from Uluru. 'Dear Son, in the desert, on a clear night, if you know where to look, you can see the planet Saturn. The word planet derives from the Greek and means wanderer. Saturn is named after the Roman god who devoured his own son. Forgive me.'

GABRIEL *looks at* ANDREW.

Forgive me. (*Beat.*) You let people go, Son, I have let people go all my life. I have run away from love... (*Beat.*) I don't know what all these things mean. It's not much. It's hardly anything at all. I can only tell you that somewhere at the end of this mess is where you belong. (*Pause*.) And now it's time to eat that fish before the world ends.

He leaves for a moment.

The ancestors watch ANDREW *as he wrestles with the weight of his mysterious past.*

As GABRIEL YORK *enters with the splendid fish on a platter. He lays it on the table and all the ancestors look at it with hunger in their eyes.*

ANDREW. It's beautiful.

GABRIEL. Listen…

They all look up… hearing the same thing in their own time and place. And for this one moment they are joined across time and continents.

The rain has stopped.

The End.